Animal World

Lizards

Donna Bailey

STECK-VAUGHN
LIBRARY
A Division of Steck-Vaughn Company

If you look carefully on a warm day,
you might see a lizard
sunning itself on a dry wall.
Don't make a noise or frighten it, or
the lizard will whisk out of sight.

2

Common lizards have four legs, a long tail,
a short neck, and eyelids that move.
They need the sun's heat in summer to
keep their body warm.
During winter they hide in burrows to
stay warm.

At night, lizards hide in the cracks
of big rocks or under stones.
At sunrise, they leave their hiding place.
At first a lizard puts only its head out
to warm in the sun.

Later the lizard finds a rock or bank
where it can lie in the sun.
It flattens its body against the rock to
catch as much of the sun's heat as possible.
The warm rocks under the lizard also help
to heat its body.

Lizards eat spiders and insects.

They spend a lot of time looking for food.

Their sharp eyes keep watch for their prey.

Their forked tongue flickers in and out.

Their moving tongue can taste an insect's trail.

Lizards don't have outer ears like ours.
But they have very good hearing.
Thin skin on the sides of their head
picks up even the smallest sounds.
A lizard can track an unseen beetle or
spider just by listening to it.

Lizards have enemies.

Many birds like to eat them.

Some lizards can change color
to hide from enemies.

This common lizard has a pattern of
spots and stripes to help it hide.

Some lizards can break off their tail
when they are attacked.
After the tail breaks off, it wriggles rapidly.
The lizard leaves its tail and scurries for cover.
The moving tail distracts the enemy.

Later the lizard grows another tail.
The new tail never grows to be as long
as the first one was.

A lizard's dry skin has scales
that overlap each other.
Its skin stretches easily, especially
when the lizard has swallowed
something large.

Lizards shed their skin
from time to time.
New scales grow under the old skin.
The lizard loses the old skin
in sections.

Lizards usually mate in spring.
Sometimes male lizards fight each other
to decide which one will mate with the female.

After mating, female common lizards
carry eggs inside their body.
The baby lizards are born
about three months later.

Most baby lizards hatch from an egg.
But baby common lizards are born
inside a little bag of skin.
The baby lizards push the bags open
with their nose.

The young lizards are a darker color
than their parents.
They get lighter as they grow.
When they are a year old, they will look
the same as their parents.

16

Mother lizards do not look after
their young.
Young lizards can feed themselves
a few hours after they hatch.
They can track down prey and
can move just as fast as their parents.

Most lizard eggs have soft, leathery shells.
The shells stretch as the baby lizards
inside them grow bigger.
Female lizards bury their eggs in
a warm, damp place where the eggs will hatch.

18

When an egg is ready to hatch,
the baby lizard breaks the shell with
a special egg tooth.
The lizard loses its egg tooth
soon after hatching.

This male lizard is puffing out his throat
to show the female the bright colors
underneath his chin.
The male makes a display to attract a mate.

Lizards often display when they are
afraid or angry.
To frighten an enemy, lizards make
special movements, such as doing
pushups or waving their tail.
Lizards also hiss when they are excited.

The blue-tongued lizard opens
its mouth wide and sticks out
its tongue when it is angry.
This display makes the lizard look fierce.

Some lizards use spines or crests
for protection.
The armadillo lizard holds its tail in
its mouth and curls up into a prickly ball
if it is attacked.

This is a frilled lizard.

The lizard usually keeps the frill folded.

When the lizard is attacked, it raises
its huge neck frill and hisses fiercely.

The flying lizard uses flaps of skin
attached to its ribs to glide from tree to tree.
When the lizard wants to move to
another tree, it holds out its wings
and makes a long, shallow glide.
It can glide as far as 48 feet.

Chameleons also live in trees.
They have long, curly tails that
help them hold on to branches and twigs.
The toes on their hands and feet
are specially arranged so they can
grip the branches tightly.

26

Chameleons have large eyes that
stick out from the sides of their head.
Each eye can move by itself.
Each eye can watch a different insect.
The chameleon's long tongue has a sticky tip.
The tongue flicks out to catch an insect.

Chameleons can change color
to match their surroundings.
This chameleon looks like
a piece of bark on the tree.

The horned lizard is also hard to see.
The colors of its skin match
the colors of the sandy desert floor.
The horned lizard hides by wriggling
sideways into the ground until
only its head shows above the sand.

The largest lizard is the Komodo dragon.
It has a powerful, slow-moving body that
grows to a length of about ten feet.
It eats small deer, wild pigs, and even
water buffalo.

The smallest lizards are geckos.

The smallest geckos are less than one inch long.

Tiny hooks on the pads of their feet
help geckos run up the walls of houses.

Desert lizards need very little water.
When it is hot, they burrow into the sand
or stay under rocks or plants.
You would have to look carefully to find
a desert lizard.

Index

Editorial Consultant: Donna Bailey
Executive Editor: Elizabeth Strauss
Project Editor: Becky Ward

Picture research by Jennifer Garratt
Designed by Richard Garratt Design

Photographs
Cover: Bruce Coleman (Hans Reinhard)
Ardea: 9, 10 (Pat Morris)
Bruce Coleman: 2 (Adrian Davies); 3 (Hans Reinhard); 4 (G. Dore); 5, 14 (George McCarthy); 8 (Andy Purcell); 12, 15 (Udo Hirsch); 13, 26 (Jane Burton); 17 (Gordon Langsbury); 18 (Javier Andrada); 21 (Mark Boulton); 23 (John Visser); 25 (C. B. Frith); 27, 28 (Kim Taylor); 30 (Bruce Coleman Ltd)
NHPA: title page, 16 (L. Campbell); 11 (Stephen Dalton)
OSF Picture Library: 7 (Larry Crowhurst); 19 (Mantis Wildlife Films); 20, 29 (Michael Fogden); 24 (Kathie Atkinson); 31 (Babs & Bert Wells)
Planet Earth Pictures: 6 (Mark Mattock); 22 (Vincent Serventy); 32 (Hans Christian Heap)

Library of Congress Cataloging-in-Publication Data: Bailey, Donna. Lizards / Donna Bailey. p. cm.—(Animal world) Includes index. SUMMARY: Studies the physical characteristics, behavior, and life cycles of different kinds of lizards. ISBN 0-8114-2645-9 1. Lizards—Juvenile literature. [1. Lizards.] I. Title. II. Series: Animal world (Austin, Tex.) QL666.L2B156 1991 597.95—dc20 90-22988 CIP AC

ISBN 0-8114-2645-9
Copyright 1991 Steck-Vaughn Company
Original copyright Heinemann Children's Reference 1991

1 2 3 4 5 6 7 8 9 0 LB 96 95 94 93 92 91